My Little Blue Book

The CheezeBoy

Paperback: 978-1-959224-19-8
eBook: 978-1-959224-20-4
Library of Congress Control Number: 2022921512

Ordering Information:

Prime Seven Media
518 Landmann St.
Tomah City, WI 54660

Printed in the United States of America

**WARNING! Contains some strong
and offensive language!**

TABLE OF CONTENTS

DAGMARA

**Dagmara. Your eyes are green. You have one
of the loveliest smiles that I have ever seen.
When you smile it lights up your pretty face.
Everytime I see you my heart starts to
race. I love your boobs, your legs, your
tum. I especially love your sexy bum. I
like you so much it wrecks my head. I
would love to take you home to bed!**

With me and Tanvinder u see...
Well lets put it this way...
I was caught offside in her 18 yard box too
many times and produced a little 'un' that
I may, or may not be able to see again.

**I'm sat in my room all alone and
bored out of my skull.
If only I didn't have the flu. I could go
out, get pissed and hopefully pull.**

My workplace is shit, but the wages are worse than
someone who looks after what's in your purse.

We have 3 shifts to do. The managers aint got
a bloody clue. There's too much work to do.
It's gone to the dogs and most the chicks are
not all dogs. Some beauties there are. But it's on
my doorstep. Wish I got more respect for the
stuff that I do. I should be a trainee operator
too. My they don't give a shit about me.

ROLLER - COASTERS

My room's like Blockbuster. I've got
everything from Bambi to the Dambusters.
Some films are good. Some are shit. Some
are dirty. Some are sick. Some'll make
you wanna play with your dick/clit.
Now watching House On Haunted Hill. It's 1
you can watch and just chill. The roller-coaster
at the start looks like the Incredible Hulk
at Universal Studios, Island Of Adventure,
Florida, United States Of Whatever (U.S.A.).
I went on it in 2000. The month of
September. But no lift or parting track.
If you go on it you might fill your sack. It
doesn't just scare you. It fucking terrifies
you. Remember it's called the Incredible
Hulk. Unless you hate roller-coasters, it
won't make you the incredible sulk.

EARLY SHIFT

It's 5:20 in the morning on the way to work. Getting up this fucking early, you must be berserk. Walking past Masons who specialise in wood. All the trucks used to be **yellow**, but they're white and blue and more mellow. They've downsized too. Why? I don't have a clue?

Now getting to Marsdens who do lawnmowers. They do new ones and repair old ones. Marsdens are the best at the art of cutting grass. You can sit on some of them and drive real fast. While cutting and smoking grass.

Now at Avery Dennisen's. They used to be labels people. I heard it's not the same as when it was Atlas. Twas great fun working at Atlas. I was there for around 3 years. Had lots of fun. Had lots of beers. Me and my brother from another mother. We misbehaved like gods and got away with it, because they didn't give a shit, as long as we all printed our bit. Got too into drugs just for the buzz. But too much and my job went to the burnt floor. So they fired me by fiddling my production scores.

Now I'm at Xylem/Flyght, who do water pumps. My mates dad worked there for a few years. If he talks to you on the streets now, he will handcuff you and say you're nicked.

Now I'm standing at the crossroads. Don't know which way to look? Left or right? Up or down? I feel I have the soul of a sad and lonely clown.

Ra Ra Rakusen. Cracker of the Russian Queen.

STOP AND STARE

Stop and stare. Yesterday I got my 1st pubic
hair. It's blonde, long and curled. I'm so happy
that I'm gonna tell the whole wide world.
I've just told my friend Chuck. Now I
wanna go out and get my 1st fuck.
You don't know what this means to me.
Getting my 1st pubes at 20, just me.

**There is a ghost in my fridge...
I think it's a polter-ice.
It keeps drinking my cider and eating my food!
By heck, this ghost sure is rude.**

+ MADISON +

+++ MADISON 15/01/2008
22:20 – 21/01/2008 01:35
2 Pounds 4 Ounces R.I.P. +++

*+ IN LOVING MEMORY OF MADISON OUR
BEAUTIFUL LITTLE ANGEL. WE LOVED
YOU FOR A LIFETIME IN SUCH A SHORT
TIME. YOU WILL ALWAYS BE MISSED BY
MUMMY AND DADDY. YOU WERE A RAY OF
LIGHT. GOD BLESS YOU. SLEEP TIGHT +*

SMOKING BAN

I got to work and I went berserk. I was caught smoking last week. No-one said owt. Not a peak. I was outside having a fag and someone caught me. What a drag. The smoking ban is really shit. Don't dare go out. Not even for a bit. You can't smoke in a public, or workplace. My company used to have a smoke room. It was really ace. You had a smoke. You laughed and cried. Twas great fun being able to smoke inside.

That's all changed now. For the worst or best? They say if you smoke, you'll soon be in eternal rest. After the hearst and sooner than you think. I must admit ciggies do make you stink. But if you get caught too many times you might end up in the clink. I don't know what's worse ciggies or drink? I'll be back soon. Just need to think...

I never got done, so I think that I won. Now I don't smoke at work, which isn't fun. This smoking ban might not be so bad, but all day at work without a fag. When I'm stressed it can make me mad. But at £6 a pack, not being able to smoke as many makes me glad. It's unhealthy and expensive to smoke. But this smoking ban's no joke.

You could lose your job if you act like a nob. Being sacked for smoking would be like a smack in the gob. You could lose your home. Living on the streets all alone. Through the long, cold nights. Seeing all the frights, delights and sights. You could get hooked on drugs because of the stubs. So it maybe wiser to abide to the law. Otherwise you maybe shown the exit door.

+ HILLSBROUGH +
(BY BFAM)

+ To the 96 that passed away at Hillsbrough
on that fateful day, now looking down with
smiles so proud, you sing with us, as we sing
aloud, you help us, guide us, get us through.
I know Istanbul 2005 was down to you. And
though the future is unknown. 1 thing's
for sure... You'll never walk alone. +.

N.F.F.C.

Talking of football... In the 2007/2008
season Forest left promotion very
late... They won 3-2 on the last day.
Doncaster who were 2nd lost away.
Then Carlisle in 3rd only drew... Which made
Nottingham Forest Football Club 2nd and
through. Now we're in the Championship.
And hopefully next step, the Premiership?
I don't know how we're going to cope... As
some of our best players are injured, or have
climbed out the Forest and taken the rope.
At the moment they aren't playing
bad. But not picking up points is
making me very sad. It's that bad!

I ONCE HAD A GIRL

I once had a girl her name was T. and I loved her everyday. She's the reason I decided I wasn't gay. It started well. The best I've had! But 2 years later I'm bitter, twisted and sad. For the 1ˢᵗ few months all we did was shag. Then she became pregnant. What a drag! I was scared, upset, happy and sad. The pregnancy hormones turned her bad! She beat me, She threatened me, She strangled me, She raped me, She cheated on me. And afterwards she had no memory?

Sometimes I was in the corner shaking and crying. She'd say "what's wrong?" I'd say "your beatings and stranglings. I feel like I'm dying". She'd say "but I'd never hurt you! I'm a good girl? I'm a barrister!". Whether it was hormones? I don't know? But at many different occasions... I felt my mind or body was about to go. It affected me so badly, but I loved her so madly, that I was prepared to to leave my wonderful family!

They thought that if I stayed by her side, they were worried the police would come around and tell them that I've died. They thought she would kill me and not remember. I had to decide if it's now or never...? I've decided to stick with my family. Because living with T. did often worry me. I can't get the bad times outta my memory.

Between the really good times and the insanely bad times... Me and T. had a baby girl. We called her Addison. She looked like me, which I was glad to see, because her mum cheated on me with at least 2 x 3? Which was at least 5 more than me. Addison was born over 3 months early and after only 5 days God took her away. With an infection caused by E-Coli.

It destroyed our hearts, our souls, our minds. It's worse than anything else in the world. It really did make our toes curl. It's the worst emotion in the world, to lose a child. It ended our love. That bolt from above. It hit us when we were at our calmest and turned it into our saddest. After a few months, we'd both gone mad! Felt angry, bitter, cheated and sad. We'd tried to stay together. But as they say "Nothing lasts forever?".

I'm all alone at my family home. I live here now. I am all alone. My mind Isn't better. I'm not good. God I wish I had some more bud. I tried to pull the other day. But at the back of my mind are the bad memories of T. All this happened in just 2 years! But I'm still living in fear! The end is near?

Oh sexy salacious Miss Plum.
When I asked her which way she had come.
She answered "by train".
I replied "come again" and she did
several times on my thumb.

"INCHES"
(BY CHEEZEBOY
AND BFAM)

I gave her "inches 1" she said it's coming on.
Keep on, keep on my darling John.
I gave her "inches 2" She said it's coming
through. Keep on, keep on my darling John.
I gave her "inches 3" she said it's hurting me.
Keep on, keep on my darling John.
I gave her "inches 4" she said it's hurting more.
Keep on, keep on my darling John.
I gave her "inches 5" spunk began to rise.
Keep on, keep on my darling John.
I gave her "inches 6" spunk began to mix. Keep on,
keep on my darling John. I gave her "inches 7" it
felt like heaven. Keep on, keep on my darling John.
I gave her "inches 8" midwife at the gate.
Keep on, keep on my darling John.
I gave her "inches 9" nappies on the line.
Keep on, keep on my darling John.
I gave her "inches 10" out popped Ben. He said
you dirty bastards and popped back in again.

MARY HAD A LITTLE LAMB SECTION

Mary had a little watch, she swallowed it
one day, now she's taking laxatives to pass
the time away, but as the days went on and
on, the watch refused to pass, so if you want
to know the time, just look up Mary's ass.

Mary had a little lamb, she took it to
a wedding, then she tied it to a garden
post and kicked it's fucking head in.

Mary had a little lamb, she tied it
to a pylon, 10,000 volts went up it's
arse and turned it into nylon.

Mary had a little lamb, it had a touch of colic, she
gave it brandy twice a day and now it's an alcoholic.

Mary had a little lamb, so her father shot the
shepherd and turned her into minted Mary legs.

Mary had a little lamb, it's fleece was
white as snow, and everywhere that Mary
went, the lamb was sure to go.
It followed her to school one day, which
was against the rule, it made the children
laugh and play, to see a lamb in school.

END OF MARY HAD A LITTLE LAMB SECTION

NEVER EAT YELLOW SNOW.
IT COULD MAKE YOU ILL.
YOU NEVER KNOW?

NEVER PUT ANYTHING HOT
IN A CHOCOLATE TEAPOT.

THINK BETTER
WITHOUT DRUGS
27/06/2008

Do I think better without drugs? Sometimes I
do. Sometimes I don't. Sometimes they will work.
Sometimes they won't. I've done many over the
years. Some are good. Some are bad. Some make
you horny. Some make you sad. Some make you
happy, feeling the vibe. Some make you feel that
you've just died. Some make you paranoid. Some
make you trip. Some make you totally utterly
flip. Some will be the end of you. Some maybe
the making of you?

Like I said I've done a few. Mainly smoke.
Sometimes lines. Sometimes pastes. Sometimes
pills. Sometimes trips. Sometimes shrooms.
Sometimes crystals. Sometimes crack. Sometimes
I wish I could take it all back. But I'm glad to tell
you all I've never done smack. I never would and
I never will. I'd rather overdose on sleeping pills.
I know some smackheads and some are not very
nice. Don't make friends with them. Think twice.

They rob to get their next hit. But really if you think about it... Their lives are quite shit. They take from their friends, strangers and family. So don't trust a smackhead 'coz it could be a double whammy. I've heard it's the best 1 of them all. The best buzz in the world.

If you get hooked your life maybe fucked. You could turn to crime . Maybe do some time. You could end up putting your, or someone else's life on the line. You could O.D. You could end up selling your body. You could get H.I.V.

To tell the the truth I personally would rather have a cup of tea. Just give me a spliff and that'll do me.

Done acid now wow, wow, wow. It's the no1 for me. But don't take too much, seriously. Had methadone now but never again.

I see the Croats croacked 1-4 England. Walcott hat- trick and Rooney's 1st goal for 11 months. Babies come out quicker than that. They 'ad a man sent off too, for an elbow. Joe Cole got hurt tho. Revenge is sweet. Bring on Wembley. 3 Lions on a shirt. Jules Rimet still gleaming. 42 years of hurt. Never stopped our dreaming.

**There was this young lady from Ealing, she
had this peculier feeling, she laid on her back,
opened her crack and pissed all over the ceiling.**

Once I've had a shower, got dressed and dry.
I'm going to skin up, go outside and get high.

EARTH STORY BY ME
31/07/2008

I wonder if all this rain is the earth crying, because of what man has done to her? She maybe in pain because of all the violence, greed, sacrilidge and descecration. She is alive. She breaths air, farts gas and bleeds oil.

She has good times like at the beginning, when there was only 1? She gets angry with floods (Noah), earthquakes and storms. She spits fire (Pompeii). She's still growing (Everest). She's getting hotter (global warming, man made or not). She's getting wetter (ice-caps melting)

She's being robbed and emptied quicker than she can replace. She's being made unstable by us (gas, oil, coal, wood). Her immune system is down. She gets more colds and temperatures than she maybe used to. She can't breath. Her lungs are struggling (trees, less trees means less air, more pollution and hotter and filthier atmosphere).

She's being poisoned and choked (landfill sites, toxic waste, war). Her fire and brimstone materials are disappearing, along with her magnets, strengthening, vitamins and minerals (periodic table). She may not be able to produce some of them again, you know.

And what do we do to help? More cars, more guns, more trees (less trees), more wars, more bombs, more planes, more people, less animals and more pollution to make more money. When there's no more oil Mad Max will walk the earth.

But she will have the last word, the last laugh. But when and how is anybodys guess? This will become Mother Nature and Gods Country again. But how, where and when will the revenge surely come? She already did it during the ark and the dinosaurs.

She has some very bad times also. 1 of her worst could be now? She's running on empty (oil, gas, coal, water, wood) She's getting too hot. Her air conditioning is dying (trees, ice-caps melting).

She will heal eventually, but it all depends on us humans giving her a helping hand, before it's too late. We should start by giving as well as taking. Why can't we all get on like 1 big happy family and be free?

Gaynor you're an angel who's special to me.
Please come round my house and sit on my tree.

Twinkle twinkle massive knob.
How she likes it in her gob.
When the end begins to twitch. She
takes it out the spiteful bitch.

MAN - FLU
25/09/2008

I've been off work for 3 days with the man-flu.
Changed my sick days to holidays, yippee-ky-a-
motherfucker-whoppee-doo. It wasn't good being ill.
I was on flu-powders for 6 days and no drink. Too ill
to wash and eat. God did I stink? Wish I was strong
like bat-fink and my wings like a shield of steel.

Went back today and it felt the same as every
week. This aint no game. What a shit job I do, it's so
damn dull. You'd enjoy it more being a landfill site
gull. You can have a laugh with some of the staff. But
others just moan and smile less than the Mona Lisa.

The best part of being at work is, some of the
Eastern European women are so fit it drives me
berserk. I don't know some days which 1 I want to
shag 1st. It drives me berserk the women at work, as
they all have blokes, which aint no joke.

They love them so, they won't let go, so they all
say no. I've tried it on with quite a few. But all the
women say is I'm flattered, but I don't like you in that
way. Adios sweetheart. Have a nice day.

Just met Charly, he's very nice.
He made my eyes water and my face go numb.

Woke up, got outta bed. Snorted a
couple of lines into my head.
Oh, oh, oh, oh.
My nose started to bleed. That's not good.
No, no, no, no.
So I rolled a spliff and smoked some
bud. It made me feel good.
Yeah, yeah, yeah, yeah.

I NEED A SPLIFF

I need a spliff. I'm holding out for a
spliff, till the end of the night.
It's gotta be long. It's gotta be strong and
it's gotta make me feel high. I need a spliff.
Doo, doo, doo, doo . Doo, doo,
doo. doo. Aah, aah.

GROUP

I wanted to join a group when I was younger and
call it Cheeze and the Rolling SmokeFlakes, or
Cheeze and the SmokeFlakes, or Rolling Cheeze,
or the CheezeRalites, or the Rollin' CheezeFlakes?
Instead I ended up in a dead-end job at
Bluekins Print Group. Life can be so unfair
to a sensitive, loving, caring, slim white
man, with a beer belly and fair hair. I
might be over there, or there, or there.

MY EX
25/09/2008

I find it even harder these days to pull. I've always struggled over the years. Not much confidence or money. Big ears. Don't drive. Do drink. Do drugs. Not hung like a mouse. Not hung like a horse. I also live at my parents house. I'm nearly 30. I like cats, but I'm not sure about children at the moment?

My only child Addison died earlier in the year. She got E-Coli and only lasted 5 days. My ex beat me up. Had me arrested. Then shagged my brains out. I loved her too much. It got that bad we were made homeless by my mum because of my ex (but mum was right).

We lived in a Beeston hotel for over 3 weeks. All we did was fight. We couldn't eat. I missed a lot of work. That hotel turned her into the devil. It was the scariest time of my life. She nearly killed me and I still wanted her to be my wife.

Lived in my bezzie mates house with her for only a week. After that we were out on the street. But at his house we were touched by God. This is dead serious so don't be a nob. We both had weird dreams. We read a dream book and the book said we were going to win money and have a child. We got a mortgage on our dream home. The day the pregnancy test said yes we saw a glowing fish on the neighbours wall (It's a warning or a blessing apparantly). The day after the room felt warm and had an amazing vibe. For 3 days no-one fell out and the area my mate lives was calm and quiet for the whole time.

Think what you may but it all went Pete Tong and I cancelled the house. Then we went to hell in the Beeston hotel. Both of us. Then it calmed down again. We split up and got back together again. Then just past Christmas her waters broke. 11 days in QMC later, baby wasn't here. We went back home and I went back to work.

Then our little angel Addison was born. She was a little fighter, but E-Coli got her and took away our daughter. Our bright hopes were turned into no hopes. We were doing so well too. We'd re-built some bridges back. We had a lovely funeral with songs and hymns at Bramcote.

After the big earthquake in England? The good times had turned to bad times yet again. We finally finished after the police had been called yet again. Even coppers said she was bonkers and she scared us. Because of my ex, I sacrificed everything that I'd ever owned in my life, to that point. I've done this as to not see my ex again.

My family and friends finally got through to me. She left some pills at my bezzie mates. They are for Schizophrenia only!She told me they were to help her sleep. When she took them she was pleasant and mild. When she didn't, she became psycho, violent and wild.

Now after all of this my head is battered and my emotions are in tatters. That's why I find it harder these days to pull. But this chapter in my life certainly wasn't dull. The throttle and throttling were on full.

NEITHER HERE NOR THERE
28/09/2008

My room is now bare. God this aint fair. It's not as if I don't care. My belongings have now gone to the house of my ex. My life is shit. What the fuck's next? Most my possessions have all gone, but why did this happen? What went wrong?

Okay so I cheated once, but so did she. She shagged at least 5 other guys, aswell as me. She carried on cheating as if she was free. For crying out loud, she was engaged to me. She acted like a bitch and called my mum an evil witch. My mum aint bad, which makes me very glad.

My ex was mad, which makes me sad. All her problems were caused by her abusive dad. He beat her up when she was just a kid and now when she meets someone they have to get rid. She isn't bad, but what is sad is, because of her dad she is very mad. She aint got many friends, unlike me. Gotta stop writing now as I'm bursting for a pee. Ahh that's better, now my bladder doesn't hurt. Now where was I?

Yes my ex is very berserk. She thought I was seeing a Polish girl from work. This isn't true. She didn't have a clue. I've been there for 7 years and not had a single screw, from anyone there and that's true. The only friends she made, just wanted to be mates so they could get laid. It probably worked knowing that girl, as she's 1of the biggest slappers in the world.

All I did was buy her a drink and a couple of hours later I was tickling her pink. I didn't even have to think about what to say or do. She just opened her legs and said lets screw. It was my 1st shag for several years and I was like, I don't see why not, thankyou, whoppee-doo. So I put it in and shagged her silly until all the spunk had left my willy. Then we both went to bed and when we woke up she gave me head. Then I went down and sucked her clit and later that day, she let me cum all over her lovely tits. It was the best sex I've ever had with my ex and not getting any now is driving me mad. I'm struggling to pull now as I'm bitter, lonely, depressed and very sad.

It's bad enough having a paralysed dad, who had a Stroke which aint no joke. It caused a blood clot in his brain, which paralysed his left side and causes him lots of pain. It happened over 4 years ago, but exactly how we don't know. He worked down the Pit and he was in the T.A., who exposed him to gas and chemical warfare on a training day. He's smoked all his life and been the leader of the 1st Colwick Scouts and for over 40 years, my mum's been his wife. He now lives in a care home, sleeping in a room being all alone. I get sad everytime I see my dad.

When my dad had his stroke we rang 999 4 times and then finally an ambulance arrived after over 40 minutes. What a joke. If they arrived earlier the damage would've been smaller. Which makes me mad.

Our N.H.S. is poor, un-reliable and dis-organized. The government should be ashamed and feel bad. It's not the doctors and nurses fault. They do a great job. But the government are greedy, uncaring, corrupt and mad. They need a big smack in the gob for being such greedy nobs.

Britain used to be great, now it's a sorry state. Is it too late, or is it all down to fate? I don't know but I do care. What happened to us is so unfair. We're neither here nor there.

NATIONAL
POETRY DAY

So today is national poetry day whoppee-doo, horay, horay. I don't know what to write. In 3 more hours I'll be working all night. Then at 6am I'll get my fix by having a spliff to make me high. Then it's Friday morning. I'll be going to sleep and saying goodbye. The weekend starts after that.

Having some beers and hopefully shagging some girls twat. After I cum I'll put it in her bum and then spray her tits when I'm done. That's my idea of having some fun. England winning at football would also be nice. But not as great as winning thrice. It all depends on the throw of the dice.

I could also watch my black cat Millie chasing mice. But she's more likely to get some woodlice. There's lots of cats and a shortage of mice. There are more cats than dogs round our way. So you hear meows instead of barks and see lots of kids pissed and stoned on the parks. All this trouble after it gets dark. There'll be broken glass where children play. Screams instead of laughter, because tomorrow's just another day.

I wish the new generation would behave. As I'm worried about bumping into a group of them, being beaten up, stabbed and put in an early grave. I wish they had more respect. But broken families, credit crunch, greed, corruption, carnage, no discipline, lack of love. Nobody cares, what do you expect? This world certainly isn't perfect.

This life of mine is so bizarre. I'd love to remove breasts from a bra. Then put in my hard dick and make her cum. Sorry gotta go now. Here comes my nephew, sister and mum. Goodbye for now everyone. Practise safe sex by using a condom. So cheery bye everyone.

Remember keep it real, have lots of fun and remember girls don't all like it up the bum. And some of them don't even swallow cum. I feel horny now and need a wank. I'm worried about my finances in the bank. I wish the government weren't such planks. If you enjoyed this poem, many thanks.

There once was a Duchess in Bruges,
who's quim was incredibly huge.
Said the King to this dame as he thunderously
came "mon dieu! apres moi! le deluge!".

In matters penile and testicular,
my mistress is very particular.
Her great predilection is for an erection,
that keeps a precise perpendicular.

There was a young lady from Brighton who
thought that her hole was a tight 'un.
Her boyfriend said "love it fits like a glove".
She said "yes, but you're not in the right 'un".

The saintly young vicar of Bude went
sleep-walking totally nude,
arriving by chance at a fancy dress dance,
won prizes for being most rude.

WORLD CUP WARM UP.
WORLD CUP MESS UP.
WORLD CUP COCK UP

We did win thrice. Which was very nice. And scored lots of goals did England. We played really well, which was really swell. We gave them hell. We beat Andorra 0-2 in Spain. It wasn't a good game. But 3 points all the same.

We then beat Croatia 1-4 in their back yard. They played like they were tubs of lard. Twas in September. Twas a night to remember. But 3 points all the same.

We then beat Kazakhstan 5-1 at Wembley. Borat will certainly remember thee.

We then beat Belarus 1-3 in their Country. Now there's no need to worry. But 6 points all the same.

This happened in October, which is my month. This month has lots of umff. We scored 14 goals. They all played like sausage rolls. We let in 3 which is not a worry. We got 12 points outta 12. We should be on the top shelves.

I'm 30 now, holy cow. I'm getting out. I'm going bold, but I feel younger than that. Now where's that geezer I need to see about the freezer?

Have we got the right Italian manager for the job? At least he's no Swedish or ginger nob. He seems to have given the players a smack in the gob. I'm chuffed to bits about that, as they are overpayed and underplayed twats. Fabio Capello has brought us up from the bottom of the sink.

Now are the 3 Lions on the brink? Is there going to be a Trophy to remember thee? Or is it going to be same old England and they go cold turkey? I don't know how South Africa 2010 is going to go? Sorry got to go now. I've got to answer the radio! I'm a Libra, the number 20 and I'll be seeing ya!

We beat Germany 2-1 in a World Cup warm up, which was fantastic, with half the team gone. We looked balanced, dangerous, comfortable, solid and played as 1. Watch out football the 3 Lions are back. Fabio won't be getting the sack. We look good in attack and defence. But still with moments that make you whince. Against Germany we made a mistake. A mix-up with the ball and Germany scored. But our heads didn't fall. We carried on playing well as if the goal was nothing at all. The Germans kept attacking a solid defensive wall. Terry made an error and as skipper stood tall and headed in the 86th minute winner, to cheer us all up.

Get ready South Africa the 3 Lions are coming. To hopefully beat you all. Attack, shoot or pass, score, win. I hope England are the cats that get the cream. At least England are playing like a team. 11 players playing as 1. I hope all the hurting and waiting will soon be gone.

South Africa went very wrong. Copello was sacked. Lost 4-1 to Germany. We got cheated out of it. Rooney and Lampard scored before half-time to level it at 2-2. But the whistle blew.

Officials aint got a clue? They disallowed Lampards goal. They said it didn't cross the line. It was at the back of the net. Officials were blind. Officials made a massive mistake. England couldn't forget it. Second half Germany made the most of it and knocked us out.

Same old England. Same wounded Lions. The hurt goes on. Officials did us wrong. World Cup warm up. World Cup mess Up. World Cup cock Up. The 3 Lion reds were robbed by an Officials blunder. It makes you wonder. What a blunder. 3 Lions were robbed by an Officials blunder!

FOOTBALL'S FULL OF GLORY, HOPE AND DESPAIR

So Notts County aren't very good. Which makes me sad because I was a Junior Magpie when I were a lad in the 1980's. I used to go to most the Home Games with me mate and his dad. We went to Tottenham, Middlesbrough and the old Wembley 3 times (2 wins, 1 defeat).

They had a good team back then, with Tommy Johnson, Craig Short, Dean Yates, Kevin Bartlett and Steve Cherry. Some of the times were really merry. The gaffer was no jaffa. He was Neil Warnock. With Jimmy Syril and Derek Pavis on the board. At least he wasn't some weirdo in a frock. Knock, knock, knock...

It's 7:20am, just finished my nightshift. Now it's time for a gem, Derby V Forest in the F.A. Cup 4th round tonight. I'm going to bed now. I need some sleep. Going to the Starting Gate with my bezzy mate to hopefully see the reds score 3 and go to the F.A. Cup 5th round. I'd even bet a pound. Goodnight. God bless.

This week of mine I've had some stress. It's exactly a year since my daughter Addison was born and then died in 5 days. I handled it well which made me proud. It's been an emotional week, so to speak. I lit 2 candles, a white and black to remember Addisons short life and death. Things like that mess with your head.

Like I said earlier, I have to rest my head. Get ready for the Local derby F.A. Cup tie. Come on let me be. I'm gonna sleep sound. Sheep 1. Sheep 2. Sheep 3. Football's full of glory, hope and despair. offside flag over there.

ENGLISHMAN

An Englishman is someone who works with Polish people at a British company. Who uses Russian oil and comes home in his German car, wearing a suit made in Sri Lanka, a shirt from China and shoes from Thailand. He brings home an Indian take-away, opens a bottle of Italian wine and drinks it while watching the 6 o'clock news on his Japanese television, while texting on his South Korean phone. Then he pops to the pub for a few pints of Spanish, Australian or Belgian lager, British cider, or Irish stout.

He snorts a couple of lines of Colombian cocaine and says to the barstaff "this country is going to the dogs". He then walks home, lights his British cigarette with his American lighter, then goes to sleep in his Swedish bed. Then finally, when he wakes up, he has some Danish bacon on French bread with a cup of Brazilian coffee and he smokes Dutch weed. Then he chases the dragon with some Afghan smack.

One dark mornin' black as nite, I was woken
up so full of frite, rite behind me I cud hear
a noise, which drenched my soul with fear,
with tremblin' hands I switched the lite,
my buttocks clenched extremely tite, I
turned and screamed for what I saw...
It was what I'd shagged the nite before!

FIDDY SCANN

He's fiddy scann. The man with the plan. If he can't scan it no-one can. He works at Bluekins world, mad house print, where you work really hard. It's run by desperate dan's in blunderland, by tubs of lard.

After you're paid, you can't afford a maid, or to get laid. Your bills come out. Your money sprints and after all that you're skint, like a twat, having to live off sewer rat, or worse still, bruce wayne bat.

1 speed's gone, we're down to 3! What will be? Is someone else coming with another plan?

I'm sorry folks. I've cooked the yolks. I don't wanna be rude, but I need food to get me in the mood for bed. I need to rest my head, so goodbye folks, I'm very tired and I really can't wait to get wired. He's fiddy scann.

SNOWMAN
12/02/2009

T'other week, weather was bad, but snow makes people happy and not sad. Went to bed. It was a cold, dry and clear night. When I woke up in the morning everywhere was snow- white.

Walking to work at 05:20 there was snow aplenty. I nearly slipped, what a fright, but putting my walking-boot footprints in the snow was a great delight. I was the 1st person to walk on there.

Built a snowman on thursday, february 5th and this morning at 07:00 thursday february 12th he's still here. He's a bit shrunken though 8 days later. So there's still a snowman in back garden heaven.

The world's shortest fairy tale... Once upon a time a guy asked a girl "will you marry me?". The girl said "no" and the guy lived happily ever after... He rode motorcycles and sailed fast boats and went fishing and played lots of golf, cricket, rugby and football.

He drove lots of fast cars and flew planes and helicopters and shot guns. He bedded lots of girls and had lots of children and made lots of money.

He drank lots of beer, cider, wine and spirits and took lots of drugs.

He left the toilet seat up and farted and wanked whenever he wanted...

The end!

All this hurt and all this pain.
I think I'm gonna go insane.
All this bad aint doing me good.
My life's a mess. It aint no good.
It's crazy now and I feel crud.

8 MG TARS
18/06/2009

Well what a season Forest had. Staying in the Championship by 7 points gave me a reason for a bit of cheer. After the last 2 years I'm definitely not queer. I need a beer. I've shed a lot more than just 1 tear.

My mind is fucked up. I only seem to get really bad luck. Is life really full of this much muck? What a life. Still no wife. At least I've got past the stage of suicide by knife. After all this strife I'm now proper skint, unlike Larry Flynt, who likes to hustle and certainly bustle.

I'm trying to re-build my life, but can't afford to buy mars, or even go out and hopefully remove some bra's. I wish I could stop these 8mg tars, before it kills me. Or even worse, causes a stroke, like to my dad, who's now permanently paralised down his left side, very bitter, very depressed and terribly, terribly sad. All of that damage caused by 8mg tars. Aint life a real drag?

All I need is a god damn shag. Even worse is this recession. At my workplace they've laid off 49 people. Crikey that's enough to fill a steeple!

It caused a world-wide depression. People all over the world are worried about losing their homes and jobs. Because of the greedy government and banking nobs, who are still claiming huge expenses and bonuses.

While everyone with a mortgage panics about losing it all, and these corrupt politicians and bankers sit there and laugh like wankers. They've used all the loop-holes and claimed daft amounts of tax-payers money to buy a stupid little jar of honey, or to feed their dogs. While normal people are treated like dogs and made poorer, for no fault of their own. Sitting down and worrying whether or not they'll lose their homes or even jobs. But no, the MP's sit in their 2nd homes all warm and smug like spoilt nobs, who treat the tax-payer like we're mugs. Oh I hope the time will come when they have to pay their own way and be like the people of everyday.

That's when the world will become better. Is Britain really getting wetter? Hope MP's are worried sick 'coz the British people are mostly not thick. If we had half the chance we'd hit their 2nd homes with a large brick and do a celebrating dance. We're wiser now than we've ever been. We want the real truth and MP's to come clean. These silly expenses and bonuses are sometimes obscene. They should be punished, fined and sent to jail. Where they'll be treated like bitches and shagged.

They certainly won't be paying for 2 cars, but will be needing plenty of packets of 8mg tars. They should make them MP's and bankers pay their own way, for their own mistakes, instead of us and spend the tax-payers money in the correct, uncorrupted, sensible, useful and helpful ways (police, fire, N.H.S., air ambulance, lifeguard, education, military and charity). Not watching porn to get an erection.

I wonder how the tax-payer will vote at the general election? I'll be back. Time for bed. 6am start at work. I need to rest my head and sleep soundly in my snug double bed.

I'm in my garden having a spliff. My back is sore. My feet whiff. My hair is curly. My joints are all stiff. Life is crud. What have I done? I've had some fun. I've had some delight. I've also had more than my fair share of fright. Having a spliff has given me really great delight.

FUCK THIS .
FUCK THAT
29/05/2009

Fuck this. Fuck that. Hey what is that? That thing
in the sky? It looks like a bat. What's wrong? Is
Gotham City not looking pretty? What a pity.
Quick it's coming over here! It's getting
near! Quick go get me a beer. Then run to
my shed and get my cricket bat. I'm gonna
hit the twat. Fuck this. Fuck that.

GREAT YARMOUTH
14/07/2009

Well I don't know what to say. Went to Great Yarmouth last week. With Mum, Sis, Nephew and Bro-in-Law. Twas a wonderful week. We did and saw so much, whatever the weather. Twas great to get away from it all and just have fun. All of this without a gun!

Went swimming, cycling, paddling in the sea, where a grey seal popped up it's head and looked at me. Went on a roller- coaster, log-flume and big wheel. Twas so high, but it's not how it made you feel. Went to amusements and won some things.

Went to a farm in Norfolk (where Lotus cars come from) where they had animals, slides and rope-swings. Went on them with my nephew, and we were all smiles.

Went to Norwich (home of the canaries) for a day. Where they had a castle that was so big. It'd be too much to go round quick, even for the stig.

Went on the sea-front and loads of cars pulled
up. Mostly V8 Yank cars, but with some plucky
Brits. Well some of them were things of dreams.
Fit for Kings and fit for Queens.

BIRTHMONTH

I was born in October 1978. When dawn of the dead, the fury and halloween opened hells gate. It caused fright. It caused delight. What am I saying 10pm friday night. No wonder I Love horror films and the doors. I came home tripping once and was eaten by the floors.

I had a fantastic childhood. Went to London, North and South France, Dublin, Northumberland, Great Yarmouth, Wales, Skegness, Cornwall, Scotland and Spain. Then along came adulthood and along came the pain.

Aint life the trippiest game? Anymore of this and I'll go completely insane. I maybe a poet. Maybe I know it. I'm not totally sure. I really need a muse to keep my feet on the floor. Please help me God. I can't take anymore.

L . S . D .
29/07/2009

Something changed at the weekend. Dropped acid 4 times in 12 hours, but didn't see moving flowers or austin powers. It opened my mind. Helped me really, really unwind. Oh my Lord it opened my mind.It made me realise what I'd been missing in my life.

Lots of Love and a lovely wife. Instead of negativity and lots of strife. I'm still depressed. I'm very straight. All I need now is a beautiful female play and soul-mate. Not porno films and masterbate. It don't half hurt when I constipate.

The problem is though, I don't know whether I want an English girl, or a sexy Eastern European honey. I wish I had and earned more money. Aint life fucked up and funny. With mad bits and good bits and in between, lots of shits.

I feel more intune and not on the dark side of the moon. Dating some crazy, lazy English loon. We lost our Addison. I'm no longer a daddy! Just an unconfident, depressed, too shy saddy. Who's very broke (financially and emotionally). Who likes a toke. Who's life so far is beyond a joke.

All I want is some poontang to poke. A bit of dough. A lot more guts. Because I back away from everything and everyone. I turn down sex. I turn down fun. For fucks sake, I need a lucky break and not an unlucky 1.

Please someone help me, save me. What have I done to deserve all this shit. I feel like a right tit. Is it too late, or will it come, my 15 minutes where I actually won? But I personally do believe that the Beatles, dance music and especially the Doors, are the best when you're tripping the floors or stressed. So far outta all the drugs L.S.D. is the best. Last word out!

FINAL DAY
03/08/2009 23:00

Life was fine for a while, then way back when, it turned vile. I totally went completely berserk. I realised then it wouldn't work. Me and T. had, had our day. I'm very sorry T. If it could've gone a different way? With Addison dying. Too much crying. All the cheating, violence and lying. You're supposed to be a barrister. What went wrong? Who's to blame? Aint life and love a funny old game? With joy and pain, all without any gain...

Then suddenly I did acid. It changed me. Now I'm seeing in 3D and 4D. My mind feels free. I realised how, why, where and wow. Nothing now will ever be the same . I now know the deeper, darker, sexier, side of the game of life.

Please God help me, as I'm in so much strife. I really feel like ending my life, but I don't wanna do that, honestly, really. Now I'm a lot more weary. Please God almighty, Holy Ghost, Holy Spirit and Sunday roast. Bread and water. Troops to the slaughter. Why did you take away my baby daughter? There must be reasons? I do know this. Would it have been unhappy relationship bliss?

I will not know until the final day. I don't know when or whether, you'll throw me away. I hope that tomorrow is just another day. I know that I'm not gay. Gay means Happy too! But when am I gonna get another lay? I'm gagging for it and don't wanna throw it all away. Will it happen sooner or later? The clock's ticking. My life is droll. At least I'm not on the dole. I'd love a night in bed with a beautiful honey. Please give me a chance of scoring a goal. Goodbye God. Thankyou for listening. Now I know what my life is missing.

UP ABOVE OR DOWN BELOW ?
25/08/2009

Where do we go? I don't know. Does life depend on who or what we know? When they turn off the lights. Where do we go? Do we go up above or down below? I don't know where, what, who, or how, holy cow. I hope to go up above, not down below. When it all ends where do we go? Up above or down below?

I just don't know when it ends. You never know. It could be yesterday, today, tomorrow, or ages away. I don't know when it'll be the end of the day. I hate my life. It doesn't rock my world. I hate my work. I'm going berserk. I'd love to find out if my meat and 2 veg still work, because they're starting to rust.

I feel shitty. I'm suffering pain and pity. The recent past didn't last, but it's still up there staying fast. I've been reading and writing this book. Holy shit. What the fuck? Some is amazing. Some is shit. Some is funny. I hope that it makes me money. I'm now no longer a silly, unwise dummy.

HAPPY MMX
19/01/2010

Well it's 2010 and the last 2 years have been rough. I've grown my hair. It looks good. It suits me, people say. Girls are now interested, wahey! Is this the year I finally become, that grown up mummy's boy?

I feel like this is going to be the year, when I finally become, what I've always wanted to be. When I actually won. I'm not as sad as I used to be. I'm gonna get laid. Call it Plan B. I'm happier now than I've been in many a year. Now the bisexual thoughts have gone out the rear and the heterosexual thoughts are definitely here.

MMX is gonna be my year. Happy MMX. It certainly is and Forests form is certainly doing the bizz. My pain and depression are going away. Now I know my confidence is here, giving me fizz. I'm filled with cheer. I'm on the up. Now where are all them A-HH cups?

I will find them. I know I will. Just after paying the bills. I'm more positive than negative. My life is gonna be good. So Happy MMX. I'm rolling some bud

+ LORD'S PRAYER +

+ OUR FATHER WHO ART IN HEAVEN,
HALLOWED BE THY NAME. THY
KINGDOM COME. THY WILL BE DONE
ON EARTH, AS IT IS IN HEAVEN.
GIVE US THIS DAY OUR DAILY
BREAD. AND FORGIVE US OUR DEBTS,
AS WE FORGIVE OUR DEBTORS, AND
LEAD US NOT INTO TEMPTATION, BUT
DELIVER US FROM EVIL. FOR THINE
IS THE KINGDOM, AND THE POWER,
AND THE GLORY, FOR EVER. AMEN +

LIFE / STRIFE
09/02/2010

What's happened to me? I don't know. I don't go out. I'm afraid of fun. I really feel that the Devil won. I feel like doing a Kurt Cobain, if only I had a gun. I've got no money. I've got no honey. I never have 1. It's not funny. I work very hard for very little money. I'm falling to bits. My life is shit.

I'm treated like I'm a twit. I'm not you know. Not 1 bit. Is my 'fate' really meant to be this shit? I really feel like taking a hit and ending it all, bit by bit. What have I done to deserve all of this? I really feel that life is taking the piss. I'll never be happy. I'll never live in bliss. What have I really done that's bad? I don't deserve this.

I'm a respectful, bubbly, funny, decent lad, who doesn't really have a bone that's bad. Everything at the moment is making me very sad. I feel like dying. I feel like crying. My life's been insane recently, seriously. I'm not lying. It's not as if I'm not trying.

I work very hard for very little money. I'd really like to win the lottery, retire early and get behind the wheel. I'm not the kind of guy who punishes and steals. I've got a good heart. I've got a good soul. It's just, that at the moment, I feel that I'm in a black-hole.

My job I suppose, is better paid than being on the dole. I've gotta go now. As I've gotta go roll.

MY FUTURE
19/03/2010 08:00

Well I'm still in 1 piece. I guess wonders never cease. I'm still a bit nervous of various things. Now where is that bee? The 1 that stings. I hope the luck comes back, so I can complete my 'new things'. I need some birds, but not 1's with wings. I hope it'll come from good luck. I dunno what my future brings.

I'd really like to get on an aeroplane. Hopefully 1 with wings. Going to different places. I dunno what my future brings. Finding out about various people, places, cultures, foods and faiths. I dunno what my future brings.

My life's hit a lull and everything at the moment is pointless and dull. My life's hit a lull. I've lost the will to do some things. All I can see is what the past brought and haven't got any high hopes, of what my future brings.

I feel like a jigsaw, a mass of puzzles and muddles. Cloudy pieces, paranoid pieces, depressed pieces, hopeful pieces, given up pieces, doubtful pieces, missing pieces, lost pieces, happy pieces and sad pieces. Then with some pieces, it forgets and smothers. I need to find myself some lovers. I wonder what my future discovers. My only friend is the end.

My Brother From Another Mother is my greatest friend. I reckon we'll be buddies until the end. I'm going to bed now, just finished nights. Will my future and God bring me great delights? Hope my future is full of delights and not anymore frights. Goodnight God and Goodbye Addison.

I hope that when the end is upon me, I'll see you Addy, I'll be your daddy. I can tell you I really had won. Left good not bad, happy not sad, friendship not violence, rich not poor, peace not war, love not death, pleasure not pain, sanity not madness. Life's a game. It's good, bad, happy and sad.

AMEN, I'll write again. I dunno what my future brings.

IT'S STRANGE
25/03/2010 22:00

It's strange you know. I need my seeds to sow, help develop and grow. What the fuck happened? I really don't know. Some things now make lots of sense. Other things now are more crueller than they ever were before. My life at the moment really is a bore. I feel like I'm in a room with many a door. What door do I open? Does the room have a floor? Will it be life, death, rich, or poor? I seriously can't take anymore!

I feel like someone has blown off my balls. I'm already at the stage of climbing the walls. Stuck in a room with nothing but despair and gloom. It's like I'm sitting in a green four-walled tomb. I really don't think I'll ever lift the gloom. The walls are closing in, in my green room. Now where's the door? I can't take anymore. The loneliness and sadness is here forever more. I need somebody to show me the door to greatness and happiness, not loneliness and sadness. I'm border-line on the road to madness.

Look me up, bring me a cup, some money and peng, to completely start again. Stop the madness before it takes me somewhere that I really, really don't want to go. I'm there at the moment, when's it gonna go? It's strange. Life's strange you know. If's the middle word in life and that's completely true. Life's like having to solve many a clue. It's really good. It's really bad. It's also in parts, really mad. It's full of highs and full of lows. It's full of moments where you wish you'd said no and lots of places that you'd love to go. It's full of moments where you wish you didn't go.

When does the end come? Do we ever know? Until your number's called and you have to go. Does it ever become clear, when the end is here? It's strange you know. it's strange.

WELL WHAT CAN I SAY ?
09/04/2010

Well what can I say? I had a really strange trip the other day. I let in the spirits, who gave me a glimpse of how I can play. Was that it forever, just 1 special day? It changed my opinion of everything that mattered and took my mind away from the past, which made my mind shattered. I think I spoke to God and I think he spoke to me. He told me that I was a psychic rockstar who can let in the spirits, who use my body and guitar to play.

I think George Harrison and John Lennon came to me and tuned my guitar for me. I was in a trance for 4 hours. When I came too my fingers were bleeding and most my guitar strings were broken. It's nearly fixed now. I hope it wasn't a joke. I was also told that a girl called Rose was the 1 for me, who God chose. He said she was gonna come to me and we'll be very happy.

Nothing's happened yet, except regret. So if it's true, the trip that I was on, may have given me a clue, of what to become. I really don't know what to do, but I don't think it was real. I really don't know how I feel.

I nearly saw Addison. I was on the brink. I heard her running towards me. It made me think. It made me happy, when I was on the brink. God wouldn't show her to me for reasons unknown?

Then all of a sudden, I was just home alone.

HEAVENS DOOR / DEVILS KISS
25/04/2010

I've been off work for a week with a bad back. I took the week off on holiday, so as not to get the sack. I'm back on Monday, today is Sunday. My back still hurts. I need a job that pays well and involves less heavy work. I hate this life, I wish it would mend. I've stopped the drugs, because they were starting to send me round the bend.

This life of mine is so shit. I've hated my life in certain bits. I'm so lonely. Please God. Save me. Why can't I pull? Why can't I get some gravy? I want to die. I want to live. I'm glad that I stopped the spliff. I haven't been out in many a week. I've got no friends anymore. Only 1 who only comes round to score.

Like I said previously. I can't take anymore. I wish a girl would come knocking on my door. I wish I could find someone to adore. I feel so wasted and very raw. I want it to mend, because I can't take anymore. Where's mon amore? Where's j'adour? Where's my love? I wanna be swallowed up by the floor.

Like I keep saying, I can't take anymore. God help me now, or go outta the door and leave me alone here, on this insane life tour. I hate working my arse off and being so poor. I'm at the end of my tether. When will I get some good luck? Will it be never? At least last week, we got lovely, wonderful weather.

I won't take my life, as I've been reading this book and suicides have to re-live the moment they took their lives, over and over again, forever more, until St. Peter lets them into HEAVENS DOOR. Nothing makes sense. I don't even have 50 pence to my name. What went wrong in the last 31 years? Who's to blame? I'm sick of my life.

Where's the endgame? I feel like I'm in hell. I really can't tell. Did I do something bad in a past life? Was it terrible enough to deserve all of this? The only girls in my life are my black cat Millie, my mum and my sister. I feel like I've been given the DEVILS KISS, and cursed forever in my land of never, and I'm going to hell forever and ever. How much more shit is to come? It's a pain in the bum.

I feel like going on the run. But what am I running from? What have I done? All I've had is glum, glum, glum. What have I done to deserve all of this? All I want is fun, fun, fun. I feel like my life is just a shitty mess. Where are you Lord? Where is my bliss? Or am I just your experiment, for you to take the piss?

Give all this bad to someone who deserves it. I don't feel like I've done anything bad, to be worthy of this shit. AMEN, goodnight, my life is a fright. Bet some evil bastards are in great delight. Let them suffer. They never do. It's always the good people who get covered in poo. What does my future hold? I'm starting to go bold. Please God, give me a clue. I'm going to bed now.

This is your HOLY DAY, GOD. I feel like my life is through. Please give me the nod. Please show me the way. Show me what to do. AMEN for now. TOO-DA-LOO.

MY 1 ST VIRGIN SONG
09/05/2010

Writing a song isn't easy. Going into your head
to try to squeeze thee. Mixing it up, in a teacup.
Trying to make it write, to please thee.
It's gotta be easy, trying to please thee.
I'm thinking when God will help thee. I'm
figuring it out, calmly working it out, in the
shadows of truth and in the shadows of doubt.
What's life really about?
All the past screams and shouts at me. I
wanna make a record, without a shadow of
doubt. It's now getting better, I'm coming
about. Out of the shadows, with a whimper,
not a shout. All I needs now are the chords.
Guitar by the door, on the green floor.
Guitar by the door, on the green floor.
Strange things happened many years ago.
But it's going away, because tomorrow's
just another day. At the last weekend,
everything went in a good way.

Guitar by the door. on the green floor.
Guitar by the door, on the green floor.
Thanks John, George, Dusty and God,
for giving me the nod. I'm gonna be a
rocking poet, now that I know it.
Please everybody, move outta the way.
Guitar by the door, on the green floor.
Guitar by the door, on the green floor.
Turn off your mind. Here comes the
CheezeBoy ride. Please move aside, I nearly
died. I'm gonna change my way. I'm certainly
not gay, but gay also means happy. My
past was quite whappy, please move outta
the way. Tomorrow's just another day.
Please move outta the way and listen to
this, hopefully giving you emotional bliss.
I'm here to stay, till the end of the day.
Thanks a lot all of you for showing me the
way, to the path of glory, yeehaa, wahey.
Guitar by the door, on the green floor.
Guitar by the door, on the green floor.
This is my 1st virgin song, I
hope it don't go wrong.
Let's make the world better. Is it really
getting wetter? My 1st virgin song, is where
it stopped to go wrong. Teaching the kid's

was great fun. I think this maybe where
I re-started and won. Excuse the mis-
spells, may this song now be done. The 1st
virgin of many. I may have actually won.
Guitar by the door, on the green floor.
Guitar by the door, on the green floor.
Reading and writing this has
been educational and fun.
I think this is where I actually won.
My 1st virgin song. My 1st virgin
song. My 1st virgin song.

IT'S RAINING AGAIN
10/05/2010

Here I go to try it again. Is it gonna
be good? How, where and when? It's
raining again. It's cold and it's grey.
For crying out loud it's near the middle of
May! I think that it's happening, come hither
the day. I'm writing well, horay, horay. My
back still hurts, but the lighter job works,
for the same pay, at the end of the day.
This writing's coming like it's always been
there. I just didn't know how to find it. The
other day the hairdresser cut my hair. It
looks and feels better. I'm nearly there.
It's raining again. It's not sunnier or warmer,
but colder and wetter. I think now my life's
getting better. I'm full of verse and full
of poetry. I hope that it works and they'll
still remember me, forever and ever.
In 3010 will they still have music? What will
they be doing then? In 3010. It's flowing
like water. Hello Daughter. When I see thee,
will they still remember me? I'm full of glee,

happy and cheer. But beware folks don't drink
too much beer. Keep Britain tidy, look after
thee. Bins surrounded by buzzing bee's.
Make it safe, make it good. I've just
smoked the last of my bud.
Owls, birds and foxes can be heard in the
Colwick Wood. The noise is scary, the noise
is good. Lot's of nature living in the Colwick
Wood. We can make Britain great again.
We can make it good. Lets put
Britain back on the map.
Drip, drip, drip, it's the Drip of a tap. Lets stop
that drip and help equipe people who need it.
The place is alive, but it's raining again, it's raining
again, it's raining again. Way back when, way
back when, way back when. It's raining again.

OH WHAT A NIGHT
12/05/2010

Oh what a night. Oh what a shame. This footy malarky is a cruel and funny old game. I feel like I've had my heart ripped out. 22 on the pitch, what's it all about? It started well, with many a shout. Thousands of fans shouting about. Then it went wrong, which made the night very long. Blackpool and Germany were good. Forest and England were crud. What will it take to remove the thong? I feel like I'm trapped in a cube. I don't know where my life will go. What'll happen to me? I'll never know. I don't know what'll happen to me in this world. I feel like a brick that's just been hurled. My depression is going, which I'm glad about. This recession is bad, what's it all about? I've had some fun, I've had lots of pain. I've also had moments that were completely insane. Lately I've really been using my brain. I've done lots of stuff that was very lame and I've done lots of drugs, that expanded my brain. Some of the stuff, I'd rather not name, but

I'm still standing on 2 legs and still in the game. I'm going full throttle. I've now got the bottle to take the next step, but never forget. I now know that life's certainly not perfect. Most the stuff I've done in my life, I don't really regret, except some decisions, which I'd rather forget. Coming home from the pub I got really wet. This is the end of the song. I now feel I'm set to take on the world, with no regrets. Come on peops, place your bets.

I cross 1 magpie, 1 magpie crosses me.
May the Devil take the magpie and God take me.

MY LITTLE
BLUE BOOK
17/05/20

It's 6am, just finished work. Done 15 outta the
last 24 hours. I must be berserk. I feel like the
living dead. All the overtime has wrecked my
head, but worry not, I'll soon be in bed. When
I wake up, I hope not to still feel like the living
dead. I hope to wake up feeling alive and well.
A good day's sleep should make me feel swell.
I'm having a strongbow, it tastes really good.
15 outta the last 24 hours has made me feel
crud. I wish I had some really phatt bud. A hard
day's night does make you feel crud. I hope a
woman'll soon come to polish my wood. My
dreams are now fading, which aint very good.
Is this life of mine really meant to be
as it should? The sky's clear blue.
The birds are singing. The dawn chorus is
really ringing, ringing, ringing. Birds are
singing, singing, singing. I wonder what the
chicks parents will be bringing? All I hear

is birds singing, singing, singing. It's really relaxing. it's really good. It's a beautiful morning. I wish I had some phatt bud. I'm going now. This poem will end. Writing this book is my only friend. I wish God in Heaven would send me the ingredients, so I can completely mend, as *My Little Blue Book* is my only friend.

AY - UP - ME - DUCK
23/05/2010 03:20

It's been really hot. The past hasn't been forgot.
I feel like my insides are starting to rot. It's
witching hour 3am. I wonder if I'll ever see
the good times again? I'm glad I'm no longer
interested in men. I think that I never really was,
but the lack of women is the reason because.
My life at the moment has lost it's buzz. The
lack of woman action is the reason because.
I'm almost made up with a little help from this
book. I'm fed up with treading through lots
of muck. It's now a case of ay- up-me-duck.
Now I need a woman to give me a fuck.
Fuck's an olde English saying like ay-up-me-duck.
It means Fornication Under Consent of the King.
An olde Nottingham saying is ay-up-me-duck.
My mind's mending because of this book.
Hello everybody, ay-up-me-duck. I can't sleep
because it's so damn hot and I've got lots of
gas coming outta my bot. The past will never
be forgot. Now I look to the future, to find out

what I can do with my life. Get a wife. Have
lots of kids and live in bliss, not strife.
Here I go, I'm nearly there. I wanna
know what, when, how and where.
Are there really ghouls, ghosts, witches and
demons out there, waiting for you to slip
up? This is the end of ay-up-me-duck.

PIGEONS
05/07/2010

I'm forever seeing pigeons, pigeons everywhere.
They fly so high, really reach the sky.
There are pigeons everywhere. Some have
grey and some have brown feathery hair.
There are loadsa' pigeons everywhere.
They fly so high, really reach the sky. Then
like your dreams, they fade and die. On the
winds of change, they glide and fly. They
float like dreams. Like bird seeds they grow.
What happens next? Do we never know? I wish
I could fly like a pigeon, in the seeds of change,
on the winds of hope, on the wings of a dove.
I'm forever seeing pigeons. There are pigeons
everywhere. With grey and brown feathers,
floating, flapping and flying away.
I wish I could fly. This is goodbye.

I'VE HAD A THINK
08/07/2010

I'm still here with more umff and less fear.
I had a long think when I was on the brink.
Being pulled through the pipes, at the
bottom of the sink. I had a long think.
I discovered many a chink. I was also there,
nearly over the brink. All I could do was think
and sink. But I think I managed to pull the
chain, relax my brain and go through the
many stages of the feeling called pain.
I grabbed the chain. I pulled myself up to see the
light. I'm still unsure of what it's all about. It's
the end of the night and I still don't know what's
my plight. Is it good, bad, happy, mad, or sad?
My plight at the moment is a fright, but
I've got feelings of up coming delights.
This is the end of the song. I'm outta the sink. I'm
back from the brink. Goodbye folks, I've had a think.
The end's in sight. Thankyou and goodnight.

THERE'S SEX
ON THE BRAIN
09/07/2010

There's sex on the brain, it's driving me
insane. When will it come? Has it begun?
There's sex on the brain. When will
it arrive? The end of pain?
There's sex on the brain, it's driving
me insane. When will it start
There's sex on the brain, causing
me pain. When will it end?
There's sex on the brain. What do I
do? I've got a clue. Will it be soon,
and with who? What do I do?
There's sex on the brain, next to
the pain. What do I do?
There's sex on the brain. The truth is there.
The lies are there. There's yes's and no's right
over there. These decisions are making me
pull out my hair. I'm at the crossroads. What
do I do? Left, Right, Up, or Down? What do I
do? Which direction's best? I haven't a clue?

There's sex on the brain, causing me pain. Who really wants me, and what are your names? There's sex on the brain. What do I do? There's sex on the brain. Too-Da-Loo.

SMOKIN' BLUES
17/07/2010

I'm sittin' in me garden smokin' blues. I'm in
peng heaven because of the blues. It's some of
the best, give or choose. I've had quite a lot
of all the rest, and it's some of the best. It'll
stand upto the test. I'm sittin' in me garden
smokin' blues. I'm smokin' blues. My geezer
came through. He said it's good, this is certainly
true. I'm sittin' in me garden smokin' blues.
It's really 1 thing, that I cannot lose. I'm sittin'
in me garden smokin' blues. I'm smokin' blues.
It's stopped rainin' now, so I don't lose. I'm
chillin' in me garden smokin' blues. My hay-
fever's been bad, it's made me sad, but it's
not all bad. I really don't have to choose, but
I'm sittin' in me garden smokin' blues.
It's a game I win and a game I lose. I'm
sittin' in me garden smokin' blues. I'm sittin'
in me garden smokin' blues. It's a game I
win and a game I lose. I'm enjoyin' sittin' in

me garden smokin' blues. I'm sittin' in me
garden smokin' blues. I'm smokin' blues.
I'm sittin' in me garden smokin' blues. I'm
chillin' and writin' me smokin' blues. I'm
chillin' and writin' me smokin' blues. I'm
sittin' in me garden smokin' blues.

I GOT A LAY T'OTHER DAY
24/07/2010

I got a lay t'other day. My meat
and 2 still worked.
Horay! Horay! I got a lay t'other day. I did it
twice. Wahey! Wahey! I got a lay t'other day.
My meat and 2 worked good. Horay! Horay!
Now who's next and when's the day? My meat
and 2 are looking forward to the next lay.
How soon will it happen, the next lay? My
meat and 2 are ready. Horay! Wahey!
I got a lay t'other day. I'm feeling good.
Horay! Wahey! I got a lay t'other day. I got
a lay t'other day. I got a lay t'other day.

THE LAND OF YES I KNOW
30/07/2010

I'm cheery now. I'm happier too.

I know the basics now.

I do have a clue. I'm at the end of all the hullabaloo.

I see the light. It's shining bright. That glow that I

had is back in sight. Is this the end of my plight? If

it is. Here I go. I now think that I'm in the know.

I hope that I'm healed. I think that I know. I'm on

the up now. I really know. The journey's beginning.

Into the land of yes I know. It's getting clearer now.

Here I go. I'm heading into the land of yes I

know. I hope that yes is the best. I'm heading into

the land of yes I know. I'm ready for it now.

I really know. I'm in the land of yes I know.

This song is ending. Here I go. I'm

in the land of yes I know.

THE GREATER GOOD
06/08/2010

Why do we need knives? Why do
we need guns? Why do we need
wars? Why do we drop bombs?
Why do we do bad, for the greater good?
Why do we do violence? Why do we lie, for
the greater good? Boys in the hood. Lets chop
down no more wood. Lots of problems, for the
greater good. Got a girl now, who makes me
feel good. Why do we do bad, for the greater
good. Lots of problems down in the hood.
Why do we do violence, for the greater good?
Lets make it safer. Lets save the wood. Why
chop down all the trees, for the greater good?
Why carry knives and guns in the hood? Why
do we do violence, for the greater good?
What's happened to the neighbourhoods?
Where are the trees? Where's the wood? All
of this madness, for the greater good. What's

happened to society? The poorer good. All
of these bad vibes, for the greater good.
Where are we know? The greater good.
The poorer good, more like. What
happens is madness, not the greater
good. I'm going now to finish my bud.
All of this badness, for the greater good.
All of this badness, for the greater good.
All of this madness, for the greater good.
The greater good. The greater good.

21/04/2006

There's a blue moon in the green room.
When I look inside I see Keith Moon and
Pat Boone, playing a looney tune.
Then I see the White Witch on a dusty
broom, say "excuse me fella's, I've got a
blocked nose. Have you got a tune"?

21/04/2006

There's a house in Union Square. Where
there lives a March hare and a grizzly
bear. I don't know why they live there, but
they say "they always have"? But when
they were told they had to leave, they said
"no" and asked for help on the radio.
When help came it was a lovely
dame, with lovely blonde hair.
She said "sorry peops, I cannot help!"
and she was eaten by the grizzly bear.

BLUEKINS PRINT
21/04/2006

I'm working here at Bluekins Print. It's near
the end of the month, so I'm fucking skint. I
gave up dope. I'm giving up fags. But the time
at the moment, it fucking drags. I need a drink.
My mind's on the brink. I need to know which
direction to go. Whether it's North, South, East,
or West. Someone please tell me which way's best.
I need a girl, bloody quick, to cheer up the life of my
lonely dick. When will it happen? Only God knows.
As long as it's before my life comes to a close. I have
to say goodbye to you. Boxes to lift and pallets to
wrap. This fucking, shitty, scanning job's crap.
At Bluekins Print the walls are blue and the
managers aint got a fucking clue. The money's
shit. The job is too. Work here too long and it'll be
the end of you. I see the light coming through the
skylight, which means it's near the end of nights.
Most of the pallets are fucking broke, so talk
to the hand and not the bloke. You're a jaffer,
where's the gaffer? Most the staff are off sick.
Here comes Aldar with another pick. P-P-P Pick

up a pick list. A mars a day keeps the spaceman away. Welcome to fiddy forklift trucks, at Bluekins Print. The forklifts are not running, but the dodgy work still keeps on coming. Fork you! Fork off! Welcome to Bluekins Print.

BEEN TO FLORIDA
23/06/2011

Been to Florida. Spent 2 weeks in Florida
with me future in-laws, to the land of the
Doors. Spent 2 weeks in Florida with me
future in-laws, to the land of The Doors. It
was really great. The food was really good.
Weather was really, really hot. Been to Florida.
We got some fabulous storms. We got a lotta
sun. 2 weeks in Florida was plenty of fun.
With my future in-laws, to the land of the
Doors. Been to Florida. Been to Florida.

LUCY ELIZABETH
03/10/2011

I've gotta beautiful Daughter called Lucy
Elizabeth. But the relationship's gone in the
rough. But I see lots of Lucy Elizabeth.
Me and her mam couldn't agree to a plan,
so we split up as dates and agreed to stay
good mates, because of Lucy Elizabeth.
She's a beautiful girl. We've done really well.
She really is swell. Lucy Elizabeth. Lucy
Elizabeth. My beautiful Daughter.
My beautiful Daughter. Lucy Elizabeth.

THEY GROW UP QUICK (LIKE, WOW, WOW, WOW)
11/02/2012

Just had my little girl. She's the core of
my world. She's growing now, holy cow.
They grow up quick, don't they? They
grow up quick (like, wow, wow, wow).
She's starting to talk now. She's making noises
(like, growl, growl, growl). It's baby talk
starting now. She's trying to sit up and rollover,
but not quite there. She's got lovely blue eyes
and getting fairer hair. She giggles and laughs
to Mr Tumble, with her cuddly Pooh bear.
She's got lovely blue eyes and
getting fairer hair.
Emily's the saviour of my world. She's
growing now, Holy cow. She still
aint really got her eyebrows.
They grow up quick (like, wow, wow, wow).
She's the core of my world. Emily in the
sky, with lovely blue eyes and getting fairer

hair. She's my world. I'm getting there, to
fatherhood, with Emily Lizzy and Pooh
bear. She keeps me busy. When she starts
walking, she'll make me dizzy. My little
girl Lucy Lizzy. She's my world. I love my
little girl. I love her dear. Goodbye peops.
The poem end is near. Now it's time for a beer.
Little Emily Lizzy makes me cheer. She's the
core of my world. They grow up quick, don't
they now? They grow up quick (like, wow,
wow, wow). I love my little girl. She loves me.
I wonder how hard Fatherhood will be? I'll
now be finding out. What will be, will be. I
got to finish eventually. She's the core of my
world. Little Emily Lizzy bee. Let it be.

BLUEKINS WORLD, MADHOUSE PRINT

Another day at Bluekins World, Madhouse
Print. Lately I've worked loadsa' hours,
but I'm still fucking skint.
Another day at Bluekins World, Madhouse Print. I
work loadsa' hours and still end up fucking skint!

NEIGHBOURS R SHOUTING

Neighbours r shouting. Neighbours r shouting.
In the evening. In the evening. Naughty
neighbours. Naughty neighbours.
Neighbours r shouting. Neighbours r shouting.
In the evening. In the evening.
Neighbours r shouting. Neighbours r shouting.
Noisy neighbours. Noisy neighbours.

BIRDS R SINGING
20/02/2012

Birds r singing. Birds r singing.
Early morning. Early morning.
Birds r singing. Birds r singing. It's
really ringing. it's really ringing.
Birds r singing. Birds r singing. It's
really loud. It's really loud.
Birds r singing. Birds r singing. Keeping
me awake. Keeping me awake.
Birds r singing. Birds r singing.
Noisy birdies. Noisy birdies.
Birds r singing. Birds r singing. I
am yawning. I am yawning.
Birds r singing. Birds r singing.
Early morning. Early morning.
Birds r singing. Birds r singing. Just
finished nites. Just finished nites.
Birds r singing. Birds r singing. Without
warning. Without warning.
Birds r singing. Birds r singing.
Early morning. Early morning.

Birds r singing. Birds r singing.
It's no joke. it's no joke.
Birds r singing. Birds r singing.
Goodnite folks. Goodnite folks.
Birds r singing. Birds r singing.
Early morning. Early morning.
Birds r singing. Birds r singing.
At the dawn. At the dawn.
Birds r singing. Birds r singing. Without
warning. Without warning.
Birds r singing. Birds r singing. In the
morning. In the early morning.
Birds r singing. Birds r singing. In the
morning. The beautiful morning.

DADDY FUN
21/07/2012

Just had little Emily. It's getting
more fun, being a daddy. I love
Emily madly. She's so much fun.
I may have got it right this
time and actually won.
Just had little Emily. It's been so much fun.
Being daddy to Emily is hard, but fun. I may
have got it right this time and actually won.
Just had little Emily. It's been hard
and fun. I love my Emily.
I think that I won.
Just had little Emily. I've had daddy fun. Now
the journey has begun. Here I go to daddy fun.

I NEED A GIRL
19/09/2012

I need a girl. I need a strongbow.

I need a girl you know.

I need a girl to go down oh her knees and
blow, blow, blow. Until I shoot my muck.

I need a girl to fuck, fuck, fuck.

I need a girl to go down on her knees and
make me excited, please, please, please.

I need a girl, so I can shoot my muck.

I need a girl. I need a strongbow.

I need a girl badly, you know. I need a blow.

I need a blow. I need a suck. I need a fuck.

I need a girl, so I can shoot my muck.

I need a girl. I need a strongbow.

I need a girl. I need a girl. I need a girl.

I need a girl. Then I'll be truly

happy, as the days go by.

I need a girl. Yes I know.

THERE'S SLEET IN THE SKY AND A STORM WITHIN

28/02/2013

There's the watering can on top of the
glass bin. There's sleet in the sky and a
storm within. There's still a chill in the
air for this time of year. There's still a
storm within. Inside the glass bin.
There's sleet in the sky and tears within.
There's sleet in the sky and a
storm within. There's the watering
can on top of the glass bin.
There's sleet in the sky and a storm
within. The watering can is on the glass
bin. I hope 1 day that I will win.
There's sleet in the sky and a storm within.
There's sleet in the sky and a storm
within. There's sleet in the sky
and a storm within, still.

U R MY MILLIE
11/06/2013

I c your fur is burning. Eyes as bright
as stars. Running around the place.
Sometimes u can't b arsed.
U r my Millie. U r my Millie.
Sometimes u r silly. Sometimes u can't b arsed.
U r my Millie. U r my Millie.
My ageing cat, who's nearly black. I c your
fur is burning. Eyes as bright as stars. All
green and bright. They reflect the night.
U r my Millie. U r my Millie.
Sometimes odd. Sometimes funny. I wish that God
would give me some money. So I can enjoy plenty
of honey. Like Winnie The Pooh, or The Who.
U r my Millie. U r my Millie.
My ageing cat, who's nearly black. She caught
a mouse outside the house. She R.I.P.ped it in
2 and ate it all. That poor little mouse outside

the house. R.I.P.ped in 2. But why, what, snot?
The rest of the verse, I simply forgot!
U r my Millie. U r my Millie.
My ageing cat, who's nearly black.
U r my Millie. U r my Millie. U r my Millie.

THERE'S THE CHEEZEBOY
21/06/2013

In a green room with green curtains,
there's the CheezeBoy.
He's a sad boy who wants to be happy. Lately
he's been changing dirty nappies. He's a
good boy. He's a wild boy. He's a mild boy.
With a good heart and a good
soul. In a green room with green
curtains, there's the CheezeBoy.
If u meet him. If u greet him. He'll
be happy, but sometimes whappy.
Sometimes sad. Sometimes glad.
In a green room with green curtains,
there's the CheezeBoy.
There's the CheezeBoy. There's the CheezeBoy.

FEEL ROUGH TODAY

Drank 2 bottles of vodka this morning, with
2 of my friends. Feel hung-over. I've got the
bends. Feel rough today. Feel rough today.
Too much vodka this morning, with 2 of my
friends. Feel rough today. I've got the bends. I'll
have plenty of water, until my body mends.
Drank 2 bottles of vodka this morning, with
2 of my friends. Feel rough today. I've got the
bends. Enjoyed it though. I'm a pale shade of
yellow. Feel rough today. I'm very mellow. Don't
feel like saying hello. Enjoyed it though. My
head hurts. My neck hurts. Feel rough today.
I've got the bends. I can't wait until my body mends.
Feel rough today. Feel rough today. Feel
rough today. Feel rough today.

A 6 NIGHT WEEK
03/11/2013 06:30

Just done a 6 night week. What a feat. I'm
knackered now. I feel weak. 54 hours. That's
more than Austin Powers. What lovely flowers.
A 6 night week has used up all my powers.
A 6 night week. A 6 night week.
I managed to do it. They had a defeat.
I won today. I won today.
A 6 night week has left me weak. But I'll get
lots of wages from a 6 night week. It was worth
it in the end. I enjoyed it too. But 54 hours is a
lot to do. I defeated them though. Here I go.
A 6 night week was a feat. But 2 weeks
wages for 1 weeks work. To turn it
down would be completely berserk.
A 6 night week. A lot of work. But I managed
to do it. I managed to work a 6 night week.
A 6 night week. A 6 night week. A 6 night week.
A 6 night week. A 6 night week. A 6 night week.

WOKE UP THIS MORNING . I FOUND MYSELF DEAD
17/04/2014 07:25

Woke up this morning. I found myself dead.
Lately I don't know what's wrong with me head.
It's the middle of April and I've got no bread.
Payday seems too far away. I'm not Happy.
Paedo's are evil, evil, evil. We shud go medievil
on them sicko people. Especially them who are
under a steeple. Them sicko, evil, paedo people.
We shud go medievil on them paedo people.
Especially them who are under a steeple. Them
sicko, evil, paedo people. Woke up this morning.
I found myself dead. Lately I don't know what's
wrong with me head. The weather's been great
in the last few weeks. I hope summer isn't
gonna have an early peak. Things are in bud.
Colour everywhere. I keep getting **greyer** hair.
Woke up this morning. I found myself dead.
What shall I do now? Holy cow. I keep
getting **grey** in my eyebrow. I know what to

do. I'm going to bed. It'll give my head time
to rest. Somethings in life truly are blessed.
Goodnight folks. My mate got 2 double-yolks.
Woke up this morning. I found myself dead.
Happy Easter folks. I'm off to bed. Woke up
this morning. I found myself dead. Woke
up this morning. I found myself dead.

I HOPE IT DON'T DELIBERATE
26/05/2014

Just had Emily, which is always great. Her
mummy's got a new play-mate. I hope it don't
deliberate. I hope it don't deliberate, my
relationship with Emily as her daddy-mate. As
her daddy-mate. I hope it don't deliberate. My
beautiful daughter Emily, which won't be great.
Her mummy's got a new play-mate. My
beautiful daughter. My little pea. There's such
a bond with her and me. She's my power for
life. She helps me get over strife. My beautiful
daughter. My little pea. I hope they still let me
and Emily see. My little pea. My honeybee. I
hope they still let us see. My amazing daughter.
My little pea. I hope it don't deliberate me.
Or as John, Paul, George and
Ringo would say "Let It Be."

MY MIND IS RACING
27/05/2014

My mind is racing. What am I facing? My
mind is a mess. My life is dull. Am I ever
going to pull? Am I ever going to pull? The
trigger's ready. You'll have to go steady.
The trigger's ready. The trigger's ready.
My mind is racing. What am I facing? My life is
dull. I'm in a rut. My finances and confidence are
now kaput. How will I get out of this massive rut?
My mind is racing. What am I facing? Am I dead?
Am I dead? What is going off in my head?
My mind is racing. My life is dull. When
will I ever pull? When will I ever pull?My
mind is racing. My mind is racing. What
am I facing? What am I facing.
My mind is racing. What am I facing? My
mind is racing. What am I facing?
My mind is racing. What am I facing? My
mind is racing. My mind is racing. My
mind is racing. My mind is racing.

FIELDS OF GREEN . SKY OF BLUE
23/06/2014

Fields of green. Sky of blue. Clouds of white. Sun's shining through. I'm on the train going back to NG1. My kidney's are in pain. MDMA has messed with my brain.

Fields of green. Sky of blue. Clouds of white. Everywhere covered in bright sunlight. It's lovely and warm. I feel that I've been re-born. My body's screwed. My cash has gone. I'm on the train going back to NG1. I've had a laugh. I haven't won. Apparently I pulled, but the memories are gone.

Fields of green. Sky of blue. Clouds of white. Sun's shining through. Fields of green. Sky of blue. Clouds of white. Sun's shining through.

What happened on Friday night? I aint got a clue. Fields of green. Sky of blue. Clouds of white. Sun's shining through. I had a laugh. I pulled a giraffe. My mate Red said. But the memories are dead. Fields of green. Sky of blue. Clouds of white. Sun's shining through.

I'm on the train going back to NG1. To my life of pain and being alone. Fields of green. Sky of blue. Clouds of white. Sun's shining through. I'm on the train. I'm on the train. I'm on the train. I'm on the train going back to NG1.

Fields of green. Sky of blue. Clouds of white. Sun's shining through. Fields of green. Sky of blue. White fluffy clouds. Sun's shining through. Fields of green. Sky of blue. White fluffy clouds. Sun's shining through.

Just gone through a trainstorm. Just gone through a rainstorm. Just gone through a thunderstorm. Phew! Fields of green. Sky of blue. Clouds of white, grey and black. Sun's no longer shining through. When's the train due back at NG1?

BUTLIN'S WEEKENDER 24/06/2014

Butlin's weekender with my mate Red. Twas really fun. I lost my head. Butlin's weekender with my mate Red. Friday night I lost my sight. I don't remember Friday night. Seriously, really. I barely have any memory. Butlin's weekender with my mate Red. MDMA blew up my head. Twas really ace. It changed my pace. It really made my heart start to race.

Friday night I was off my face. I lost my sight. I really let Suarez bite. I really let Suarez bite. Friday night I lost my head. Lots of booze, little snooze. Lots of booze, little snooze. Friday night I lost my sight. Butlin's weekender with my mate Red. When I got home I went straight to bed. When I got home I went straight to bed. Butlin's weekender with my mate Red. MDMA on Friday night blew up my head. Twas really fun. Twas really great. Butlin's weekender with my mate Red. Twas the total opposite of being dead. Twas the total opposite of being dead.

MDMA blew up my head. Butlin's weekender. Butlin's weekender. Butlin's weekender I lost my head. Butlin's weekender at Costa del Skeg. Butlin's weekender at Costa del Skeg. Thankyou Butlin's, I'm off to bed. Butlin's weekender at Costa del Skeg. Butlin's weekender wrecked my head. Butlin's weekender at Costa del Skeg. Butlin's weekender. Butlin's weekender. Butlin's weekender at Costa del Skeg. Thankyou Butlin's, I'm off to bed. Thankyou Butlin's, I'm off to bed.

Butlin's weekender at Costa del Skeg. Lots of booze, little snooze. Lots of booze, little snooze. Butlin's weekender at Costa del Skeg. Butlin's weekender. Butlin's weekender. Butlin's weekender at Costa del Skeg. Butlin's weekender with my mate Red. Butlin's weekender at Costa del Skeg. Butlin's weekender with my mate Red. Butlin's weekender at Costa del Skeg. Butlin's weekender. Butlin's weekender. Butlin's weekender was 1 to remember. Butlin's weekender was 1 to remember. Thankyou Butlin's. Return my Kidneys and Lungs to sender!

+ R . I . P . DADDY +
29/06/2014 22:25

+++ So this is the end of *My Little Blue Book*. I've finally finished it, thank fuck. My Dad died at 3:30 this morning. What the fuck! He was okay yesterday and now he's gone a long way away. I don't know what to say. It's been a very strange day. So this is the end of *My Little Blue Book*. It's finally done now, thank fuck. Goodbye. Goodnight. Good luck. God Bless You Daddy and say hello to my little Addison. Now I've finished *My Little Blue Book*. R.I.P. Daddy. Already missing you +++

THIS IS THE END OF MY
LITTLE BLUE BOOK . . .
By The CheezeBoy
M . I . M . CheezeBooks Ltd.